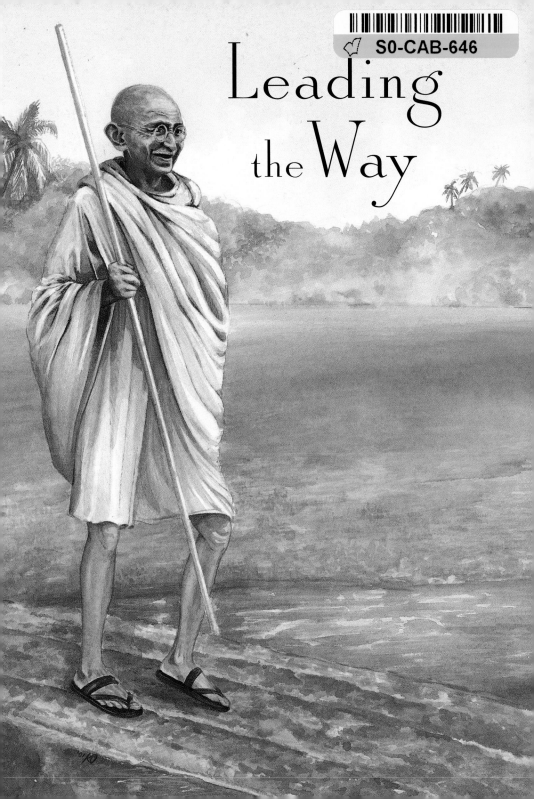

Leading
the Way

Contents

Leading the Way 4

Harriet Tubman 6

Mahatma Gandhi 10

Kate Sheppard 14

Terry Fox 18

Glossary 22

Index 23

Bibliography 23

Discussion Starters 24

Features

Have you ever heard of a railroad with no tracks? Solve the mystery on page 9 with **The Underground Railroad.**

What does the name *Mahatma* mean? What language is it? Turn to page 10 to find out.

In 1893, nearly one-third of all adult females in New Zealand signed a petition. Find out what it was about on page 17.

Terry Fox decided to run across Canada to raise money for cancer research. Discover how much money he raised on page 19.

What is the Red Cross and what does it do?

Visit **www.rigbyinfoquest.com**
for more about **WORKING FOR CHANGE.**

Leading the Way

Throughout history, many people have worked hard to improve the lives of others. Some have put their own safety in danger by helping people they didn't even know.

Harriet Tubman, Mahatma Gandhi, Kate Sheppard, and Terry Fox are only four of the world's many heroes. They came from different countries and different backgrounds, but they all had something in common. These people spent their lives leading the way to a better world.

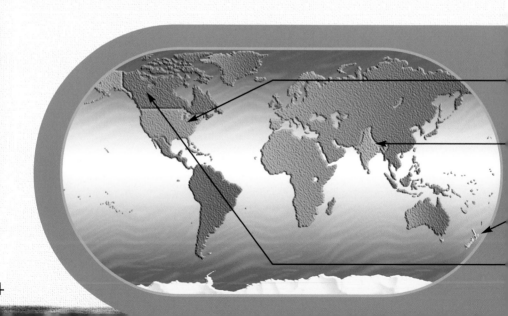

In 1893, Kate Sheppard won the right for New Zealand women to vote in government **elections.** In 1912, the women in the photo above marched in New York to show that they wanted voting rights for the women of the United States. However, it wasn't until 1920 that U.S. women won these voting rights.

Key to Heroes

 Harriet Tubman, U.S.A., helped people escape slavery

 Mahatma Gandhi, India, won India's political freedom

 Kate Sheppard, New Zealand, won women's right to vote

 Terry Fox, Canada, raised money for cancer research

Harriet Tubman (1820?–1913)

Who Was Harriet Tubman?

Harriet Tubman was born around 1820 into **slavery.** Her early life was very hard, and she was often beaten. In 1849, Harriet used her bravery and knowledge of the woods to escape.

She then became the most famous African American leader of the **Underground Railroad.** Harriet made nineteen dangerous trips, leading hundreds of slaves from the South to freedom in the North. Harriet Tubman was one of the bravest, most caring people in American history.

Harriet Tubman's Life

1820? Born in the state of Maryland in the United States

1833 Had head hurt by owner after getting in way of owner chasing another slave. Sometimes fainted from then on.

1844 Married John Tubman

1849 Escaped from slavery using the Underground Railroad. Traveled to another state.

1850 Made first trip back to Maryland to help other slaves escape. Returned 18 times during next 10 years, leading about 300 slaves to freedom.

1857 Led parents to freedom

1861-65 Was an army nurse and scout during the **American Civil War.** Helped free more than 750 slaves.

1865 Raised money to build schools for African American children

1908 Started Harriet Tubman Home for elderly African Americans

1913 Died and was buried with army honors

What Did Harriet Tubman Do?

Harriet Tubman spent her life helping other people. She often lay alone in forests all night, waiting for slaves who she would guide along the Underground Railroad. Slave owners offered a reward of $40,000 to anybody who could catch Harriet. However, she outsmarted them every time.

During the Civil War in the United States, Harriet helped more than 750 slaves escape. Since her death, Harriet Tubman has been honored in many ways.

After the war, Harriet kept helping others by raising money for African American schools. She also opened the Harriet Tubman Home for the elderly (left).

The Underground Railroad

Harriet Tubman (far left) with a few of the hundreds of slaves she led to freedom.

From 1830 to 1860, thousands of slaves escaped from slavery to live where slavery was not allowed. They traveled along the Underground Railroad. However, the Underground Railroad was not underground, and it was not a railroad! It was a secret escape trail. Hiding places were called stations. The people who gave the slaves food, clothing, directions, and places to hide were called conductors. With the help of 3,000 conductors, over 100,000 slaves used the Underground Railroad to escape.

Mahatma Gandhi (1869–1948)

Who Was Gandhi?

Gandhi was born in India in 1869. At that time, Britain's government controlled India. Like many others, Gandhi believed that the people of India should be free to make their own laws.

During his life, Gandhi helped to free India from Britain's control. This alone would have made Gandhi famous. However, it was his belief in peaceful **protest** that made Gandhi highly respected around the world.

WORD BUILDER

The name *Mahatma* means "Great Soul" in Hindi. Gandhi (*GAHN dee*) was given this name by the people of India in 1914.

Gandhi's Life

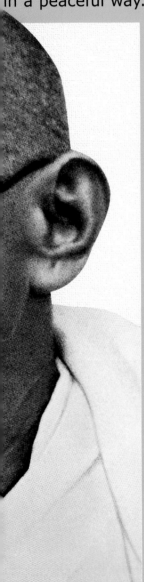

Gandhi believed that instead of fighting, people should try to change the world in a peaceful way.

1888–1891
Studied law in England

1914
Left South Africa and returned to India

1931
Traveled to Britain to meet with the British Prime Minister, the government leader

Jan. 30, 1948
Killed when shot in New Delhi, India

Feb. 5, 1948
One million people attended Gandhi's funeral

Oct. 2, 1869
Born in India

1893–1914
Worked in South Africa for the rights of India's people

1930
Led hundreds of people on a 240-mile protest march to the sea

Jan. 13, 1948
Stopped eating to show he didn't like the fighting between groups in India

11

What Did Gandhi Do?

Gandhi was a great leader of the people in India. He ran many peaceful protests against Britain's control of India. He also led marches, went on **fasts**, and spoke about equal rights for all people. Gandhi spent seven years in prison for his beliefs.

After many years, Gandhi's protests paid off. In 1947, the British left and India became **independent**. However, shortly after this, Gandhi was shot by a person who did not agree with him about freedom for all people.

Gandhi valued people much more than things. These are the only things he owned when he died. They were worth just a few dollars.

One million people went to Gandhi's funeral. To the people of India, Gandhi was the father of their country. All around the world, people were very sad about his death.

Kate Sheppard (1847–1934)

Who Was Kate Sheppard?

Kate Sheppard was born in England but moved to Christchurch, New Zealand in 1868. At that time, women around the world were not allowed to vote in their countries' elections.

Kate thought this was unfair and believed that women had as much right to vote as men. She fought for many years to win voting rights for women. In 1893, Kate won her battle and New Zealand became the first country in the world where all women could vote.

Winning the Vote Around the World

New Zealand led the way in letting women vote in 1893. Some countries followed quickly. For others, the battle was long and hard. The timeline below shows when women could vote in some countries.

1893 – New Zealand
1902 – Australia*
1917 – Canada
1918 – Germany, Ireland,
     Britain
1920 – United States of America
1930 – South Africa*
1937 – Philippines
1942 – France, Bulgaria, Jamaica

1947 – Singapore, China, Mexico
1957 – Malaysia, Zimbabwe
1962– Australia**
1990 – Samoa
1994 – South Africa**

* White women only
** All women

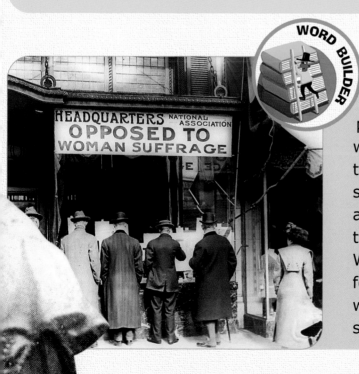

WORD BUILDER

In the 1800s and early 1900s, many people believed that women "belonged in the home" and should not be allowed suffrage— the right to vote. Women who fought for voting rights were often called suffragettes.

What Did Kate Sheppard Do?

Kate Sheppard spent many years writing notices and letters to newspapers. She held public meetings and talked about why every adult should be able to vote for the people who made laws and ran the country. She met with government leaders, and she started **petitions.**

Kate Sheppard worked for years to win voting rights for women in New Zealand. She also worked to help women who were fighting for the vote in other countries.

Around the world, people put up posters, trying to make others see why women needed the right to vot<

July 29, 1893

New Zealand Times

The largest petition in New Zealand history has been presented to the government. The petition, started by Mrs. Kate Sheppard, calls for law changes to give women voting rights. Almost 32,000 women have signed the latest petition. This is nearly one-third of all adult females in New Zealand.

E MOTHER THE VOTE

WE NEED IT

VOTES FOR OUR MOTHERS

FOOD OUR HEALTH OUR PLAY
HOMES OUR SCHOOLS OUR WORK
RULED BY MEN'S VOTES

Isn't it a funny thing
That Father cannot see
ny Mother ought to have a vote
n how these things should be?

THINK IT OVER

Printed by National Woman Suffrage Publishing Company, Inc., 505 Fifth Avenue, New York

VOTES FOR WOMEN

Terry Fox (1958–1981)

Who Was Terry Fox?

Terry Fox, a teen in Canada, enjoyed playing sports. Then, at eighteen, he lost a leg to bone cancer. Some people may have given up hope of ever running again, but not Terry. He wanted to do something big to help other people who had cancer. He decided to run across Canada and collect money for cancer research along the way.

On April 12, 1980, Terry dipped his artificial leg in St. John's Harbor, Newfoundland to begin his fundraising run called the "Marathon of Hope."

SITESEEING • PEOPLE & PLACES •

What is the Red Cross and what does it do?

Visit **www.rigbyinfoquest.com**
for more about **WORKING FOR CHANGE.**

FACTS

OSY·124

When Terry planned his run, he hoped to raise one million dollars for cancer research. He ran 26 miles every day for 143 days. When Terry died on June 28, 1981, his Marathon of Hope had raised more than twenty-four million dollars.

Terry Fox ran 3,339 miles. He raised a huge amount of money for cancer research. He also changed the way many people think about having handicaps, and he showed what amazing things just one person can do.

Although Terry died before being able to finish his Marathon of Hope, his dream did not die with him. Now every year in 58 countries, more than 1.5 million people walk, jog, or cycle in the Terry Fox Run to raise money for cancer research.

Money Raised for Cancer Research in Terry's Name

The Marathon of Hope

NADA

Thunder Bay

St. John's Harbor

Ottawa

Terry's run across Canada

1981: When Terry died on June 28, he had raised 24.17 million dollars through his Marathon of Hope.

The Terry Fox Run

Today: A total of 270 million dollars has been raised in Terry's name.

2000: 1.5 million people in 58 countries raised 21.7 million dollars.

1981: 300,000 people took part in the first Terry Fox Run in Canada and raised 3.5 million dollars.

'Even though it was so difficult, there was not another thing in the world I would have rather been doing."
—Terry Fox

Glossary

American Civil War – (1861–1865) a war between the Southern and Northern states of the United States. The Southern states wanted to keep slavery and the Northern states wanted to end slavery. The war was won by the North.

election – the process in which the people in a state or country vote for their government

fast – a time when food is not eaten. Gandhi fasted as a form of peaceful protest.

independent – self-governing, not ruled or controlled by another country

petition – a form asking for a change. People sign a petition to show they agree with it.

protest – to speak out against or oppose something

slavery – the condition of being owned by another person and working for that person without being paid money

Underground Railroad – a secret group of people in the United States who did not believe in slavery. During the 1800s, these people helped slaves escape to safety in the North. This name is also used for the secret path the slaves traveled.

Index

American Civil War   7–8

Fox, Terry   4–5, 18–21

Gandhi, Mahatma   4–5, 10–13

Marathon of Hope   18–21

petitions   16–17

Sheppard, Kate   4–5, 14, 16–17

Terry Fox Run   20–21

Tubman, Harriet   4–9

Underground Railroad   6–9

Bibliography

• Boon, Kevin. *Kate Sheppard*. Kotuku Publishing, 1993.

• Elish, Dan. *Harriet Tubman and the Underground Railroad*. Millbrook Press, 1993.

• Johnson, Ann Donegan and Steve Pileggi. *The Value of Facing a Challenge: The Story of Terry Fox*. Value Communications, 1983.

• Lazo, Caroline. *Mahatma Gandhi*. Dillon Press, 1993.

Petition

The women who have signed the petition below ask the government of New Zealand to extend voting rights to all women

Mildred Smith   21 Ball St
Kate Williams   86 Garden Ave
H Armitage   The Mews, East St
R J Fisher   91 Wandering Pl
Helena B Paul   3 Grosvenor Tce
Nina Black   89 India Pl
Maude Elmchapel   13 Palace Quay
Violeta Text Black   Number 3 Crampton Court
C Wallace   7c Nagpur Tce

Discussion Starters

1 Harriet Tubman dared to help other slaves escape. Why do you think she put herself in danger to do this?

2 Today, it seems strange that 100 years ago most women around the world did not have the right to vote. What would you have said or done to help women get voting rights?

3 Very few people would push themselves to run across Canada. Do you think Terry Fox was an amazing person? Why or why not?

VOTES FOR WOMEN